Anxiety

The Ultimate Beginner's Guide To Rewire & Retrain Your Anxious Brain & End Panic Attacks - Daily Strategies To Finally Overcome & Stop Your Constant Anxiety, Fear and Worry

By *Freddie Masterson*

For more great books visit:

HMWPublishing.com

Get another book for Free

I want to thank you for purchasing this book and offer you another book (just as long and valuable as this book), "Health & Fitness Mistakes You Don't Know You're Making", completely free.

Visit the link below to signup and receive it:

www.hmwpublishing.com/gift

In this book, I will break down the most common health & fitness mistakes, you are probably committing right now, and I will reveal how you can easily get in the best shape of your life!

In addition to this valuable gift, you will also have an opportunity to get our new books for free, enter giveaways, and receive other valuable emails from me. Again, visit the link to sign up:

www.hmwpublishing.com/gift

Table of Contents

Introduction 1

Chapter 1: HOW THE ANXIOUS MIND WORKS 4

    Neurotransmitters and Anxiety 4
    Anxiety and Brain Activation 6
    Anxiety and Hormones 7
        Adrenaline/Epinephrine 8
        Thyroid Hormone 8
    Panic Attacks and the Brain 10
    More Connections 10
    Treating Anxiety When it Has a Brain Cause 11

CHAPTER 2: THE NEUROSCIENCE OF FEAR 12

    What Goes in your Brain When you are Afraid? . 12
    Is Fear Innate or Learned? 14
    What Are People's Top Fears? 16

CHAPTER 3: DEALING WITH ANXIETY 18

    Why is Anxiety so Powerful? 19
    Using the Power of an Anxious Mind 21
        Control Anxiety, Don't Let Anxiety Controls You! 22
    Be Patient! 23
    Just Observe 24
    Trust your Anxiety 24
    Always Trust yourself 25

Meet your Anxiety 26
Clear your Filter 28
Accept Uncertainty... 29

CHAPTER 4: HOW TO GET RELIEF FROM WORRY, ANXIETY, AND FEAR 31

Why is it Hard to Stop Worrying?....................... 32
Rule #1 - Create a Worry Time 33
Rule #2 – Is the Problem Solvable 36
Rule #3: Challenge Anxious Thoughts 40
Cognitive Distortions that Add more to Anxiety, Stress, and Worry 43
Rule #4 – Accept Uncertainty 45
Rule #5 – Be Aware of Others 47
Rule #6 – Exercise Mindfulness..................... 49

CHAPTER 5: FOODS TO HELP YOU BEAT ANXIETY 52

Involve Foods Rich in Omega-3 Fatty Acids ... 52
Include Healthy Amount of Complex Carbohydrates 53
Opt for Chamomile Tea................................... 54
Consumer Foods High in Tryptophan............. 54
Eat Vitamin B-Rich Foods 55
Incorporate Protein at Breakfast 55
Be Hydrated 56
Foods to Avoid... 56
Reduce the Amount of Omega-6 Fats............. 57
Avoid alcohol.. 57
Reduce Caffeine 58

  Avoid Simple Carbohydrates and Sugars 58
  Manage Food Sensitivities 59
  Incorporating Other Activities to Manage Anxiety Naturally 60
  Take Supplements 60
  Exercise 61
  Get Enough Sleep 66
  Visit your Physician 67

Conclusion 68

Final Words 70

About the Co-Author 71

Introduction

It would be surprising to know that your brain is the source of your anxiety. It's not only that anxiety manifests in things that cross your minds, but it also affects your brain chemistry in such a way that it can alter future thoughts and therefore influence the way your body operates.

As you know, anxiety can be a troubling disorder. You can feel physical symptoms even though you may not feel anxious which can cause you to act upon life events as it reinforces itself on your behaviour.

This book, "Anxiety: The Ultimate Beginner's Guide to Rewire & Refrain Your Brain to End Panic Attacks, Fear and Worry (Neuroscience, Beat Panic Attacks)" will guide you with the following:

- ✓ How to control your conscious mind and unleash its power to your advantage over anxiety issues

- ✓ Manage and control panic attacks, anxiety, worries, and stress

- ✓ Understand how proper dietary lifestyle can help you combat anxiety.

This book further caters to the need of individuals who are prone to anxiety attacks due to the nature of their work, a previous traumatic experience, especially during the childhood, and people who have a psychological disorder indicating a lower emotional quotient (EQ).

Also, before you get started, I recommend you **joining our email newsletter** to receive updates on any upcoming new book releases or promotions. You can sign-up for free, and as a bonus, you will receive a free gift. Our *"Health & Fitness Mistakes You Don't Know You're Making"* book! This book has been written to demystify, expose the top do's and don'ts and to finally equip you with the information you need to get in the best shape of your life. Due to the overwhelming amount of mis-information and lies told by magazines and self-proclaimed "gurus", it's becoming harder and harder to get reliable information to get in shape. As opposed to having to go through dozens of biased, unreliable and un-trustworthy sources to get your health & fitness information. Everything you need to help you has been broken down in this book for you to easily follow and to immediately get results to achieve your desired fitness goals in the shortest amount of time.

Once again, to join our free email newsletter and to receive a free copy of this valuable book, please visit the link and signup now: www.hmwpublishing.com/gift

Chapter 1: HOW THE ANXIOUS MIND WORKS

Anxiety can occur at any time in the course of a lifetime, and it can be forged over the years of experiences; however, some individuals are born with an abnormal imbalance in generating certain neurotransmitters, which is a substance that controls specific bodily functions, and emotional aspects. Whether or not your DNA is prone to anxiety disorders, it is essential to know that it is highly treatable.

Neurotransmitters and Anxiety

Inside the human body, we have these chemical substances that send messages to your brain about how you perceive things. These transmitters are linked to anxiety due to hormonal changes including Serotonin, GABA, and

Norepinephrine. Even dopamine plays a vital role as it provides a calming effect on those who are suffering from anxiety symptoms.

The cause and effect of the production of neurotransmitter are hard to determine, and it's often impossible to distinguish a poor neurotransmitter balance resulting from life experience and a neurotransmitter balance resulting from genetics. Both of which can occur in a person living with anxiety, and there are some cases that both can be responsible for the anxiety symptoms.

Anxiety and Brain Activation

Anxiety disorder consists of two different parts, and it's possible that an individual with anxiety may be affected by one or both parts.

For the first part, there are mental/nervous thoughts and verbal worries these. The other part is physical, as a racing heartbeat manifests it, lightheadedness, panic attacks, sweating and other physical signs.

Researchers have discovered that people with anxious thoughts have shown more activity in the left brain every time they felt nervous while those that have expressed physical symptoms have demonstrated right brain activity.

A recent research study of arachnophobia has monitored and analyzed the reaction of participants who "self-identified" as experiencing spider anxiety as they expected to confront their fear with direct exposure to the insect. It was found in the results of the said study that to certain individuals their dorsal anterior cingulate cortex

(ACC), thalamus, and insula got more active than those who didn't have expressed a fearful response to the idea of confronting a real spider.

Another study conducted by the University of Wisconsin-Madison also discovered that people with generalized anxiety disorder appeared to have a weaker connection between the white matter of the brain and the prefrontal, and anterior cortex of the brain. In comparison to those without generalized anxiety disorder in which the result appeared to be more significant.

The following will explain the different ways that anxiety can activate the brain.

Anxiety and Hormones

A hormonal imbalance can lead to anxiety which can also affect the brain chemistry as well as the neurotransmitter production and general emotional balance.

Thus, if there appears to have an imbalance in the hormones, anxiety can arise. As such, we will analyze here below the hormones that may significantly affect the brain.

Adrenaline/Epinephrine

This hormone is considered one of the most common causes of anxiety. This hormone is released once the person is in a fight-or-flight mode. It can contribute to an increase in the heart rate, muscle tensions, and much more. In other cases, anxiety and long-term stress can cause damage to your ability to control adrenaline, therefore, adding more anxiety symptoms.

Thyroid Hormone

Thyroid hormones regulate the production of Gamma-aminobutyric (GABA), serotonin, and norepinephrine and distribute them to the brain. Therefore, an overactive thyroid can increase the risk of developing anxiety. Several hormones may cause stress and any change in the brain chemistry can augment the production of hormones which could lead to further anxiety symptoms.

Panic Attacks and the Brain

Studies confirmed that those with panic attacks have overactive amygdala. Though it's not clear what causes this over activity, the fact remains – that particular area in the brain is in control of the panic attack experience.

More Connections

Studies divulged that when anxiety is left untreated, the dorsomedial prefrontal cortex, hippocampus, anterior cingulate, dorsolateral prefrontal cortex, and orbitofrontal cortex all appear to diminish in size. So the longer your anxiety is left untreated, the smaller and weaker they become.

What is interesting is the fact that not only do these changes affect anxiety symptoms, but it also creates anxious thoughts. People suffering from anxiety assume that their way of over thinking of over-analyzing situations is purely natural, but in reality, the brain contributes to that type of negative thinking.

Treating Anxiety When it Has a Brain Cause

It's also common for people who are having a difficult time with an anxiety disorder to feel depressed as a result of the way anxiety is interfering with their lives. However, with the right treatment, the human brain is incredibly adaptive as it can respond positively in overcoming worries and any negative thoughts.

There are many paths to overcoming stress and getting your life back. By being consistent and have patience with yourself. Using the proper relaxation tools will allow you to control your overall anxiety.

CHAPTER 2: THE NEUROSCIENCE OF FEAR

You may enjoy watching horror movies – zombie apocalypse, murder mysteries, action adventures and suspense thrillers. But what draws you towards these horror movies when you know these will only cause you to feel scared?

What Goes in your Brain When you are Afraid?

Every time you are exposed to scary situations, you are automatically turning on your fight-or-flight response. It is in this state that your body produces adrenaline hormones which can give your supernatural strength otherwise it would not be possible in a typical situation.

In 2008, The Journal of Neurology published that flooding the brain with dopamine also affects behaviors suggestive of fear and paranoia in rats. Since dopamine is also associated with pleasure, when this hormone is released during scary scenarios along with the so-called "rush of adrenaline and endorphins," it can lead to an elevated or high sensation. Some people enjoy this type of feeling.

Most people don't like going through terrifying situations. When we are watching suspense thrillers and horror movies, our brain quickly processes the information transmitted and perceives that the threat is not real. So when our senses trigger a fear response, like we are thrown out of our seats in a fun ride, our brain immediately recognizes that there is no real danger, but instead we are in a safe and secure situation.

Though psychologists were not able to identify a fear center in the brain, the amygdala which nestled between the temporal lobes is somehow responsible for processing scary situations or threats. Animals with damaged amygdala are seen to be tamer and show fewer fight-or-flight responses.

When threats are introduced, there is a neural activity observed in the human amygdala, along with an increased heart rate.

In 1995, a study in the Journal of Neuroscience backed up the fact exposing the dominant role played by the amygdala in the fear response. A study of a woman, simply as named "SM," with a rare genetic disorder, "Urbach-Wiethe" disease which caused the shrinkage and calcification of her amygdala was conducted. As observed, SM showed no signs of fear, and she could not recognize the expression of fear in everyday scary situations even when surrounded by deadly vipers.

Is Fear Innate or Learned?

Some fears are innate-like the fear of your first performance before a large audience even though you know you can perform well. Though, you should perform before a smaller crowd. We depend on fear for survival, or otherwise, we would be conditioned to fear things that are not scary.

In the results of the "Little Albert Experiment," a famous 1920 emotional conditioning experiment, was found that fear can be learned. A 9-month old baby named Albert was conditioned to fear furry objects in the same way that Pavlov experimented with dogs.

In this experiment, Albert was exposed to animals and furry objects. The experimenters would give the child a white rat to play with, which the baby enjoyed. At this point, Albert did not display any unpleasant reaction towards the animal. After succeeding multiple trials, the experimenters would strike a suspended steel bar with a hammer, causing a loud noise as Albert would attempt to touch the rat. The act was repeated several times until the animals and objects that were once a source of joy and curiosity had become a trigger of fear to the baby. It eventually developed a fear of all furry objects including fur coats, a rabbit, and even Santa's bearded mask to the child.

Our fears can also depend on previous experiences during our childhood, particularly those that were traumatic. For example, dog bites and attacks are traumatic events and can have emotional consequences that can affect the victims for years.

Every time our emotion runs high, the chemicals in our brain works to strengthen the memories of the situation. It's like storing snapshots of events that

happened at that particular time.

What Are People's Top Fears?

A 2001 survey conducted by Gallup among 1,000 American adults disclosed that about 51% of the participants are afraid of snakes along with public speaking, heights, confined spaces, etc. Responses showed that women are more likely afraid of reptiles and insects while men are more fearful of going to the doctor.

One crowd-sourced survey conducted by Yahoo out of 20,000 volunteers found a slightly different result in 2015. The top three phobias shifted to fear of height (acrophobia), fear of spiders (arachnophobia), and fear of enclosed spaced (claustrophobia). Also included in the top ten:

- Fear of deep waters (thalassophobia)

- Fear of public speaking (glossophobia)

- Fear of needles (trypanophobia)

- Fear of butterflies (Lepidopterophobia)

- Fear of objects with irregular pattern of holes (Trypanophobia)

CHAPTER 3: DEALING WITH ANXIETY

Anxious thoughts can be powerful. In fact, it can out-run, out-power, and out-smart your logic and reasoning. So what will happen if you can utilize the power of this potent mind and harness its strength and power to work for you rather than against you?

At the most basic level, anxiety is an emotion. It can quite be shocking, but fear and anxiety are important emotions. When it comes to human survival and achievement, anxiety and fear motivate us to take necessary action. Therefore the body instantly response by producing adrenaline hormones which make us act quicker.

However, we know, any excess is nearly always bad

for the health. So when the brain gets oversensitive, it puts the body on a high alert level even when there's nothing to be alarmed. Thus, how our body response to anxiety disorder serves no useful purpose. This is called a false alarm.

Why is Anxiety so Powerful?

Anxiety is supposed to keep us safe. It is a call to action response of fight or flight when we are in the presence of an immediate danger, as our body will automatically begin to prepare us to attack the threat or to escape from danger. As anxiety is automatic and instinctive, the ability to perform the necessary actions can ensure our survival, but in some situation, it can cause us serious prejudice. When we become excessively anxious, our mind often takes the form of unproductive worrying. Moreover, intrusive thoughts and worrying in this sense represents an unsuccessful attempt to control the danger at hand. Then, we begin experiencing distress from not taking the proper action. We then fall into this vicious circle of anxiety.

As we learned above, we know anxiety is based on the reality of a situation, but may end up sabotaging what the person needs to accomplish. Sometimes, anxiety can crop up which, to others, seems out of proportion to the actual situation. On the opposite, anxiety can play a necessary role for survival and optimal functioning which is how things get done by responding to it. If we learn how to master our mind; the "good anxiety" can benefit us by rectifying or ameliorating certain situations.

With constant practice, there are some aspects of anxiety that you can use to find calmness in the midst of turbulence.

Changing mindset involves small patterned steps. The road to recovery may be long and rocky, but they are more likely to experience significant, life-altering changes as a result of the skills you will put into practice every day. Note that your mind has been used to reflect a certain way and it can take a while before you can break these habits.

Don't try to take drastic measure

s all at once as it will only cause you to give up. Take one step at a time and for a short while – small but important steps! Remember, any time you are out of your comfort zone, you going to feel anxious. So, be kind to yourself!

Using the Power of an Anxious Mind

When anxiety is the power of the mind against the mind, then you can use it as your greatest asset rather than an obstacle. In fact, most of the time anxiety means something great is going on and that you are moving through new challenges. What builds confidence in you? The answer is simple: Accomplishment. Your mind is powerful, use it to your advantage. Don't spend your time looking back at a life that was "safe" and "comfortable." You will not regret the things you do in life so much as the things you DON'T do.

Control Anxiety, Don't Let Anxiety Controls You!

Be where you want and not where it wants to lead you. Anxiety uses a solid collection of "what-ifs" and "maybes."

Try anchoring yourself by opening up your senses. Be mindful of your senses. What are you most afraid of really? A great tool is to go back to memories of when you felt seriously anxious about a new element of your life. How did things turn out? Chances are everything was just fine, and it's really useful to remind yourself of this. Be comfortable with what is presently happening rather than anticipate what might happen. If you feel uncomfortable, limit the time – dedicate as much time to fully explore and experience things as they are in the present.

As you do this, you are strengthening your ability to pull back your anxious thoughts to live to moment.

Get into this Mindful exercise every day for as long as you can – the longer, the better. The bottom line here is to keep exercising your mind to positive thinking and rewires to new challenges. Such experience is healthy and your brain will surely appreciate it!

Be Patient!

Thoughts and emotions come and go. Not one of these stays forever, so always remind yourself that no matter how you felt at a specific moment or what comes into your mind will always come by.

Experience the presence of being fully present without feeling the need to push away your thoughts and emotions. No matter how strong these thoughts and feelings seem to be, you are always mightier and stronger than any of these. You are always more resilient so don't hurry them up while passing. Instead, let them stay longer so you can observe them and realize their purpose in your life. Once you do, they will quickly pass away.

Just Observe

You don't need to engage with your anxious thoughts. Delving deeper into your anxious thought is a waste of time and strength. Detach yourself from your anxious thoughts by taking the time to auto-analyze your over-thinking through scary situations. When you understand the things that terrify you, you can find the sources of fears.

To illustrate this, imagine that you are in the midst of a storm. Instead of trying to control the direction of the mighty wind away from you, you can picture yourself watching the storm through a window and knowing that soon, it will pass.

Trust your Anxiety

Your strong consciousness and thoughtful mind will try to put these anxious feelings and put it in context because having the idea that they are not attached to anything can make you feel even worse.

You might feel stressed about the things that cause your worries – which is common in anxiety. You start thinking if it is a sign to protect yourself from something bad that might happen.

Practice to calm yourself down by taking a deep breath as soon as your anxiety arises. It's not easy, but as you do, you'll soon be able to master your thoughts and not believe the message that anxiety brings to your emotions.

Anxiety comes as a warning and not a prediction. You need to feel the safety and security of what that means to you.

Always Trust yourself

Trust that no matter happens you are in charge of your emotions. That might not feel real with you at the start, just go ahead with it and see what you can experience from this. As said before, it is a learning process, and it might take time.

The very underlying cause to anxiety, worry, and stress is the fear that you won't be able to cope.

However, don't underestimate yourself.

You are strong and resourceful, so you will always cope with anything that is thrown at you. This has happened many times before, and you have proven yourself that you are capable of coping with anything – rejections or taking wrong decisions. It's just a matter of accepting them and letting go. It had happened in the past, though dressed differently, but yet, you were able to move forward.

Meet your Anxiety

Sometimes, the more that we try to fight or change something just to feel good, the more it stays the same. The energy that we put into that is exhausting. In this case, try to tell yourself not to think of pink gorillas and see how it works!

Anxious thoughts take you a lot of precious mental space and even draw on our emotions, imaginations, focus, and thoughts. The more we try to control them, make sense of them, the more that they feed into our anxiety.

Try to accept being with your anxiety, without trying to change it. Accepting your anxious thoughts and feelings doesn't make them stronger or stay longer. In fact, they cease when you stop feeding them with your energy.

What you have your focus on becomes potent. So the more you focus on something, the more it grows and flourishes to expand. Therefore, try to stop yourself from pushing your anxiety away. Without forcing your anxiety to go away will bring you an understanding of it so you can deal with it.

Exercise accepting your feeling as they are for about two minutes. This is not easy but this is powerful. Start with little bits and work up from there. If you can work on it for more than 10 minutes (sitting with your anxious thoughts like they are something natural), then the better it is for you. After a few minutes, give them your full attention and try transforming them into something else. See how it feels when you're ready and works on it longer.

Clear your Filter

Experiences from the past as well as messages have their way of changing the filter through which we view life, and the world is living. This is how it works for us regardless of the presence of anxiety in our life.

Try to see moments and experiences as though they occur for the first time in your life even when you have experienced them too many times in the past and yet, no one will be exactly like what you are facing in the present moment. Notice the difference between what is happening now and what has happened before.

Every, the time you experience it, you are changing for the better – more brave, wise, strong, and more capable of dealing with your anxiety though there are times when you are more anxious and more worried.

Be open to new possibilities that come with this new experience because that's what it is, a whole new experience!

Let's say you have a painful breakup with a long-time relationship, so there's always this tendency to hold on back from opening your heart to a new relationship. A new relationship with a new individual can feel too risky for you and this is understandable.

For you, staying away and avoiding people is a move that will keep you safe and secured. But somehow, this will take you away from possibilities that are just there waiting for you to find them. Growth can happen when we choose to open up ourselves to what is coming rather than avoiding new experiences just because we are greatly affected by what has happened in the past.

Accept Uncertainty

Anxiety can easily cause a stir because the future is always uncertain. Not all things can go according to plan and the more we try to control every situation, the more we should realize that we have little control over it.

Try to let go of the need to be certain at all times even just for a moment. Though this can be hard to accept especially for people who are control freaks, you need to start surrendering to the uncertainty. Experiment with trying to let go of the need to control the present moment, the past or the future, and this includes controlling the people around you. If you can lean to your uncertainty and take the time to tolerate it, the less control it can have over you.

By constantly experimenting with the different strategies you will soon master over your anxiety.

Your first few tries won't bring much change as they're like drops of water in a bucket. Same thing will happen to the next, and so on. Things won't be noticeable at the start, but as you continue to use them regularly, eventually, you will be able to have more capacity to harness the strength of your wild but beautiful mind to make it work more in your favour.

You will soon realize and understand that you will always have what it takes and that your anxious thoughts and feeling will simply pass away like a bad weather day.

CHAPTER 4: HOW TO GET RELIEF FROM WORRY, ANXIETY, AND FEAR

Worrying can be helpful when it spurs you to take action and solve a problem. When you're preoccupied with the "what ifs" and "worst-case scenarios," then this can become a problem. Unrelenting doubts and fears can be paralyzing. They can sap your emotional energy, send your anxiety levels soaring, and interfere with your daily life. However, chronic worrying is a mental habit that can be smashed and transformed into something useful. You can train your brain to stay calm and look at life from a more positive perspective.

Why is it Hard to Stop Worrying?

Worrying is never an enjoyable activity, so why would someone not stop worrying? The answer to this lies in the belief you have about worrying.

If you believe that constant worrying will cause your anxiety to be completely out of control, damage your health or drive you crazy, all these will add up to your worries and keep it going far. It's just like when you worry about getting to sleep, the more you stay awake.

When you worry about why you can't sleep, this keeps you more awake. The same things work with worrying too much on your worries. Conversely, on the positive side, you may believe that positive things help you to avoid bad things. However, positive beliefs on worrying can even result in more damage as it is tough to break the habit of worrying if you believe that it can help you. To put a stop to worrying, give up your belief that worrying serves a positive purpose.

It's hard to stop the worry habit once you believe in it. You must somehow realize that worrying is the problem and not the solution so as to regain control of your anxious mind.

Rule #1 - Create a Worry Time

Isn't it hard to be productive in your daily life when troubles and worries are dominating your mind? So what must you do?

Telling yourself not to worry doesn't work most of the time – if it is, it won't last long. You can be able to distract your mind from these anxious thoughts for a moment, but not for long. You just can't banish those anxious thoughts and feelings for good. When you do this, you're even making them stronger and more persistent.

Test this for yourself. Close your eyes for a moment and try to picture a pink gorilla. Once you see this pink gorillas pop up in your thoughts, stop thinking of whatever you do for the next hour. Just don't think about this pink gorilla! But how can you do it when these pink gorillas keep popping in your mind?

Why Stopping Them Doesn't Work?

When you tried to stop these thoughts, they backfire because your mind forces you to focus your attention on the very thought you want to discard. You are always watching out for it and this what makes it more important. However, it doesn't mean that anxiety is uncontrollable. You can control anxiety by using a different approach. Instead of trying to get rid of your anxious thoughts, try to dwell on them longer but don't let yourself get affected.

How to Postpone Worrying

Create a "worry period." Set a time and place to focus on your worries. It must become a routine schedule. So if you choose to worry in your room, let's say between 3:pm-3:20 pm. The earlier, the better so you don't have to be anxious during dinner or before sleeping time. During this time set for your worries, you may think of all the worries locked up in your mind. But for the rest of the day, make sure that it's worry-free!

When anxiety strikes outside of the worry time, just take note of it and set it aside to continue with your day. Remind yourself that you have a specific time set aside for this alone. So there's no need to worry about it at this very moment.

Go Over your Worry List

When your worry time comes, go over your list of thoughts that have been worrying you. If they kept ion bothering you, then allow yourself to indulge with these worries but only for the time allotted for it. If these anxious thoughts don't appear to be important anymore, cut your worry period short to be able to enjoy the rest of the day.

Postponing worrying is, therefore, effective as it breaks the habits of dwelling on worries when you've got other things to do. Don't suppress, struggle, or judge the anxious thought, but rather postpone it for a later time. As you develop the ability to postpone your anxious mind, you'll soon realize that you have more control over them than you think.

Rule #2 – Is the Problem Solvable

Try asking yourself if the problem is solvable. According to research, while you are worrying, you are likely to feel temporarily anxious. While you are thinking about the problem, it distracts you from your emotions and makes you feel like you accomplished something. However, we know that worrying and problem-solving are two different things.

While in problem-solving, we are trying to evaluate a situation and come up with concrete solutions and then put the plan into action, in worrying, this rarely leads to a solution. No matter how much time you spend thinking about those worst-case scenarios, you'll realize that you're still you're not prepared for them when they come.

Distinguish what worries are solvable and what aren't?

Once a worry pops up into your mind, you can ask yourself whether that problem is something you can solve. To know, the following questions can guide you.

- Is it is just imaginary?
- Is the problem something that you're facing at the present moment or just an imaginary what-if?
- If the problem is an imaginary what-if, how likely it is to happen? Is your concern realistic?
- Is the problem solvable or is it out of your control?

Solvable worries are those which you can take action right away. Like for instance, you're worried about your bills, then the best solution for that is to call your creditors and asks about a flexible payment option. On the other hand, unproductive unsolvable worries are those which you can't do something – like, what if you acquire a deadly sickness someday?

When solvable worries strike, you can then brainstorm on them. List down all possible solutions you can think of, but try not to get too hung up on looking for the perfect solution. Try focusing on the things you can change, rather than on the circumstances or realities that are far beyond your control.

After evaluating all the possible options, make an action plan. To start your plan rolling, do something about the problem and you'll be much less worried.

Dealing with Tough Worries

When you are a chronic worrier, the large portion of your worries seems to be unsolvable. Worrying helps you keep your thoughts busy worrying rather than allowing yourself to be troubled with the underlying emotions. But still, you can't get away with your anxious emotions.

While you are attending to all those worries, your feelings are temporarily locked up and suppressed. However, as soon as you stop worrying, they all bounce back.

And then you start worrying about what you feel. "What's wrong? Why am I feeling this way?"

But what if the worry isn't something you can solve? If you're a chronic worrier, the vast majority of your anxious thoughts probably fall in this camp. In such cases, it's important to tune into your emotions.

Worrying helps you avoid unpleasant emotions.

When worrying, you are thinking about how to solve the puzzle rather than allowing yourself to feel the underlying emotions. But you can't push your emotions away. While you're worrying, your feelings are temporarily suppressed, but as soon as you stop, they come back. And then, you start worrying about your feelings: "What's wrong with me? I shouldn't feel this way!"

Embrace your Feelings

It seems scary at first to embrace your anxious feelings because of your negative beliefs about them. We always believe that we need to be constantly rational and in charge of your feelings. You must not feel negative emotions like anger, wrath, fear, resentment, etc.

However, emotions are just like life that is messy. They aren't always pleasant nor always make sense. However, feeling positive or negative is all part of our being human. As long as you can accept that they are normal. As well as part of how we are as humans, then you can experience them without really feeling overwhelmed and you can manage them to your use to your advantage.

Rule #3: Challenge Anxious Thoughts

Once you suffer from worries and chronic anxiety, there's a great tendency that your outlook on life is negative and for you, the world may appear dangerous that it is. To illustrate, every time you overestimate the possibility that things will turn on their worst scenarios, you also discredit your ability to handle life's problem and assume that it will always fall on the first sign of trouble. This attitude of yours is recognized as *cognitive distortions*.

Cognitive distortions are part of patterns of thinking that were long stored up in your thinking and had become automatic that you are not even aware of them. To break these negative thinking habits, you need to retrain your brain to stop the worry and anxiety they bring to your brain. Though cognitive distortions are not real, it's not easy giving them up.

You can begin by identifying a frightening thought and try to be detailed as possible as to the things that scare you or cause you worries. Instead of taking these thoughts as facts, view them as mere hypotheses that need to be further tested. As you examine and challenge your worries and fears, you will soon develop a more balanced perspective.

Question the Anxious Thought

- What is the proof that the thought is right? Or not right?

- Is there another way to look at the situation is a more realistic and positive outlook?

- What is the probability that what scares you will happen? If the possibility is low, then what are the probable outcomes?

- Is the thought helpful? Will the worrying help you or causes to hurt you?

- How can I sympathize with a friend who is worried?

Cognitive Distortions that Add more to Anxiety, Stress, and Worry

All-or-Nothing Thinking

You tend to look at things in black and white and nothing in between. Meaning, you think like this, "I'm a total failure once I fall short of other people's expectations."

Overgeneralization

From a single traumatic or negative experience, you assume that things will happen as it did. Example: I didn't pass the test. Even if I get another one, I will fail again."

The Mental Filter

Tends to focus on the negative thoughts while trying to block out all the positives. You can easily notice the one negative out of the hundreds of positives because the mind filters the positives.

Diminishing the Positive

Easily come up with reasons when the thing doesn't come up to the expectation like, "I did well on the examination, but it seems I'm not the proctor's favorite."

Jumping to Conclusions

You are quick to make wrong interpretations and judgment in the absence of evidence. You can act like a mind reader or a fortune teller.

Catastrophizing

You're always expecting the occurrence of the worst-case scenario.

Emotional Reasoning

You believe that the way you feel reflects the reality.

Labeling

You label yourself based on mistakes and also perceived shortcomings.

Should and Should-Not

You are binding yourself to a set of strict rules of what you should do and shouldn't do. You likewise will impose a penalty on yourself if you failed to follow this strict rule.

Personalization

You are assuming responsibility for things and situations beyond your control. Example: "It's because of me that he died!"

Rule #4 – Accept Uncertainty

When you have this inability to tolerate uncertainty, it will likely lead you to worries and anxieties. Chronic worriers just can't stand unpredictability as well as doubts. This is why they tend to indulge themselves in their anxious thoughts and feelings. They feel safer in worrying, but the feeling of safety is just an illusion. For them, they see worrying as a way to predict what is installed for the future. This is their way of preventing unpleasant surprises so they can control the outcome. However, the problem lies in the fact that it doesn't work.

When you are thinking all about the wrong things to come, it doesn't make life predictable. Focusing on worst-case scenarios won't keep them from happening, but it will surely keep you from enjoying life in the present moment. Therefore, if you want to stop your worries, start combatting your need for certainty and immediate solutions.

Accepting Uncertainty

Accepting uncertainty is the key to anxiety relief and so to be able to understand the problems of refusing to accept uncertainty in things or situations, guide yourself with the following questions and don't forget to write down your responses.

- Is there certainty in everything about life?

- If you try weighing certainty against uncertainty, how are they helpful or useful to you?

- Do you think that predicting bad things to come based on uncertainty is a reasonable thing to do?

- How would you assess the possibility of positive or neutral outcomes?

Rule #5 – Be Aware of Others

How you feel is affected by your surroundings especially by the kind of people you are in contact with, whether you are aware of it or not!

Studies show that emotions are contagious as they can affect others. Observe that we quickly can catch "moods" from each other – even from a complete stranger we just met on the road and probably would never speak to again People you spend much time with for the rest of the day will have more impact on your mental and emotional state.

Keep a Worry Journal

You may not be aware of how situations and people are affecting you. It could be that this is the usual scene occurring in your home. Now, to keep track of things and situations and how they much affect you regarding worrying, start jotting down notes every time you start worrying. Jot down the thoughts and see what triggered them. Eventually, you will realize that there is somehow a pattern.

Spend Less Time with Those that Brings you Anxiety

If there is someone in your life that seems you bring you much stress in life, start cutting back on the time that you are spending with the individual. You can also suggest establishing healthier boundaries. For illustration, try to set certain topics that are off-limits. We know the types of topics that usually trigger our feeling of anxiety.

Choose Carefully People You Confide With

When you're worried about something, and you want to share your anxious thoughts and feelings with others, carefully choose the person to whom you can confide these things. Some people can help by way of introducing positive perspectives, yet there are others who will just feed more into your worries, fears, and doubts. In the end, you will be more troubled that you are before you confided with this kind of personality.

Rule #6 – Exercise Mindfulness

Focus on the future – what might happen to you if you do or don't do it, or if something happens that you are somehow expecting in a way.

Mindfulness meditation technique can help ease the tension created by anxiety and help you break free from your worries while bringing your attention back to the present moment.

In contrast to what we have previously tackled about challenging your anxious thoughts and scheduling them to a worry-free time, this meditation technique encourages observing your anxious thoughts and feeling and letting them go without any judgment. These can help you determine where your thinking is causing you problems while helping you connect with your emotions.

Acknowledge and Observe

Don't control, ignore or fight these anxious thoughts and feelings. Instead simply observe them as if from the outside without having some reactions and judgment on what you see in the present.

Let Them G!

While you are trying to control your anxious thoughts, the more likely they are to pop up and soon pass away like those clouds moving across the sky. It is simply when you start engaging with your thoughts that you start to get stuck.

Stay Focused on the Present

You can pay attention to how your body feels, your breathing, and your ever-changing thoughts and emotions that drift across your thinking.

With the Mindfulness Meditation, staying in the present moment is a basic concept, yet it takes long years of practice before you can reap the benefits. While you are still starting with your exercises, you will notice how your mind can easily wander and get off the track.

You will feel frustrated when you minds kept on the dwelling to your worries. Instead of getting frustrated, each time, draw your focus back to the present. This way, you are reinforcing a new mental habit that will help you eliminate the negative, anxious thoughts and help yourself to get free of the negative worries.

CHAPTER 5: FOODS TO HELP YOU BEAT ANXIETY

There are a lot of foods that can reduce or manage symptoms of anxiety and there are others that can aggravate or worsen it. While a serious anxiety disorder requires medication and therapy, milder cases should be managed through the right diet. With a few modifications to your lifestyle and diet, you can naturally handle anxiety.

Studies have shown that there are certain foods with the ability to soothe your senses and can even boost your mood. Let us give you some tips on how you can tweak your diet with these foods.

Involve Foods Rich in Omega-3 Fatty Acids

Omega-3 fatty acids do not only fight inflammation but can also improve your mood, letting you cope up with stress. Furthermore, it can also help you fight off substance-abuse habits which are usually begun due to stress and anxiety problems.

Omega-3 fatty acids are pre in seafood like salmon, oyster, tuna, and mackerel. You can also get them from avocado, chia seeds, soybeans, spinach, walnuts and olive oil.

Include Healthy Amount of Complex Carbohydrates

These foods can increase the serotonin level in the brain which is responsible for balancing our mood. Having high levels of serotonin instigate a soothing effect on a person.

Compared to simple or refined carbohydrates, complex carbs contain higher amounts of vitamins, minerals, fiber. They can be found in foods like whole grain oats, brown rice, pasta, whole grain bread, quinoa, potatoes, sweet potatoes, corn, lentils, and even green vegetables.

Opt for Chamomile Tea

According to studies, chamomile tea can help reduce symptoms of anxiety. Take 3-4 cups a day for adequate results. Since chamomile has soothing properties, you can also try using it through ointments, liquid extracts, and supplements.

Consumer Foods High in Tryptophan

Tryptophan is an important amino acid in our diet. Our bodies cannot create it. Thus, we take it through the food we consume. This acid is an antecedent to serotonin, a neurotransmitter that works to balance a person's wood. Furthermore, Tryptophan promotes better sleep, diminishing the levels of your anxiety.

Tryptophan-rich foods include soy products, tofu, eggs, milk, cheese, peanut butter, pumpkin seeds, sesame seeds, peanuts, nuts, turkey, chicken, and fish. To make these foods more effective, prepare them with ingredients rich in complex carbs. This way, the carbs make tryptophan more accessible in the brain to generate serotonin.

Eat Vitamin B-Rich Foods

Vitamins B, more specifically B1 and B12, can fight anxiety by triggering your brain's production of serotonin. You can find various B vitamins in foods like poultry products, dairy products, fortified grains, cereals, dark leafy veggies, meat, and fish.

Vegetarians and older people are at high risk for vitamin B deficiency, making them vulnerable to anxiety symptoms. For this, taking vitamin B supplements may be required.

Incorporate Protein at Breakfast

Breakfast is the most important meal of the day. It is the source of energy that can fight the effects of anxiety during the day. A breakfast rich in protein can help you feel satisfied all throughout the day and manage your sugar levels.

Lean meat, Greek yogurt, cottage cheese, milk, eggs, tofu, whey protein, navy beans, dried lentils, tuna, salmon, halibut, anchovies, and sardines are foods that contain high protein.

Be Hydrated

Dehydration can greatly influence your mood and energy balance. Drink adequate amounts of clear fluids. Taking 8 glasses or 2 liters of water is a good rule to stay hydrated all throughout the day.

Foods to Avoid

There are foods that you need to avoid as they exacerbate anxiety. Here are ways to do to avoid anxiety through foods that you consume.

Reduce the Amount of Omega-6 Fats

Omega-6 fats which are largely taken from vegetables can increase inflammation risk in the brain and have been associated with imbalances in moods.

The Most common sources of these fats include corn oil, sesame oil, soy oil, and safflower oil. Try using olive or canola oil in your food preparation instead of oils high in Omega-6 fats.

Avoid alcohol

Even if you believe that alcohol has an immediate calming effect and good for your anxiety, the process of metabolizing alcohol will only lead to your feeling edgy. It will also interfere with your sleeping pattern.

Alcohol is shown to cause anxiety or panic attacks.

The maximum allowable amount of alcohol you can consume is one glass daily for women and a double of this amount for men. A single glass is estimated to be about 12 oz. of beer (about a ½ liter) or about 5 oz. of wine. But, giving up alcohol isn't easy, and it might be worthwhile before one can give it up completely to help manage anxiety issues.

Reduce Caffeine

Caffeine has a stimulating effect that can take up as much as eight hours before it wears off. In addition to making you feel nervous and jittery, caffeine can interfere with you resting hours.

Similar to alcohol, caffeine, which is commonly found in coffee and tea also triggers panic attacks and anxiety. It is also found in some energy drinks, sports drinks, and another supplement. So better stick with decaf coffee and tea to reduce anxiety symptoms.

Avoid Simple Carbohydrates and Sugars

Simple sugars and refined carbohydrates are said to have negative effects on energy, moods, and anxiety. Try minimizing your intake of the following foods as much as possible.

These types of food include sweet treats like candies, cakes, pastries, and food cooked out of white flour like plain pasta and white bread.

Manage Food Sensitivities

There are some foods and additives which are harmful to people with sensitivity to them. People who are affected can experience mood changes, anxiety, and irritability when consuming foods to which they have allergies.

The most common irritants could be soya, eggs, chicken, tobacco, wheat, and sugar.

Incorporating Other Activities to Manage Anxiety Naturally

Take Supplements

There are herbal supplements that are shown to have natural anti-anxiety like properties. However, before you add any herbal supplements to your diet, make sure that you consult your physician on this to make sure that they are safe and appropriate for you. You could have allergies to some of the components of a certain herbal supplement.

Take note of the following benefits you can gain from taking supplements extracted from herbs and other plants.

Passionflower Extract – It was discovered that passionflower extract could lessen overall anxiety.

Valerian Root – According to some studies, valerian root extract produces a sedative effect which is why it is used to aid an individual with sleeping issues. Other studies prove that it can likewise help in managing stress and anxiety.

Lemon Balm – Lemon balm can reduce stress and anxiety, but if you have hyperthyroidism, it's best to avoid it.

Exercise

With regular exercise, you can manage your anxiety as studies have shown that exercises have an immediate and long-lasting positive effect on anxiety.

The US government recent guidelines on health recommended at least 2 ½ hours of moderate-intensity physical workout for adults like brisk walking in a week and 1 ¼ hours of vigorous activity including swimming laps and jogging. You can do a combination of both for better health.

Having a regular exercise regimen is needed to help you cope with the bombardment of work-related stress and anxiety issues. If you have one, then it's good and keep it up. But for others who haven't started yet, here are tips to keep you going.

- Do jogging, biking, walking or dancing three to five times in a week for thirty minutes.

- Rather than work for perfect workouts, try setting up small goals and target for daily consistency. Walking 15-20 minutes a day is better than waiting until the next weekend for a three-hour marathon. Scientific studies suggest that frequency is most important.

- Choose a form of exercises that are both fun and enjoyable for you. Extrovert people often choose group classes and group activities while introverts often choose solo pursuits.

- Many people enjoy doing exercises while listening to music or sounds they enjoy. Download audiobooks, music, or podcasts through an iPod or other portable media player or devices to distract yourself.

- It would be more enjoyable if you can find an exercise buddy to workout together. Most often, it is easier to stick to your exercise regimen when you have to stay committed to a partner.

- Be patient while doing your exercises. If you're the sedentary type, it's typical for you to take about 4-8 weeks to adjust and feel coordinated and comfortable with your activities.

Cold Weather Exercise Tips

The cold weather must not stop you from doing your regular exercise regimen and here are tips to help you get through the cold.

- Dress in layers for your exercise, and you can remove it as you start to sweat. You can easily put it back when needed.

- Make sure to protect your hands, feet, and ears. Wear enough covering like hand gloves, headbands, and socks to prevent frostbites.

- Always pay attention to weather condition. Wind chills and rain can make you vulnerable to colds. If the temperature happens to be below zero degrees and the wind chill is strong, consider taking a break from your exercise activity and instead find an indoor activity.

- Choose appropriate clothing. As it gets dark earlier during winter, be sure to wear reflective clothing and wear footwear with enough traction to prevent falls in ice or snow.

- Also, remember to bring your sunscreen. You can get easily burned in winter just as it is in summer, so always bear in mind the SPF.

- Also, plan your route and make sure that the wind is at your back towards the end of your workout to avoid getting a chill after working out.

- Hydrate your body. Sometimes it is hard to notice the symptoms of dehydration in cold weather so drink more water or any refreshing liquids before, during, and after your exercise even when you don't feel thirsty.

- Know the signs of frostbites and hypothermia. At the first spot of their signs, immediately seek help to prevent frostbites and hypothermia.

Get Enough Sleep

When you are experiencing stress or higher levels of anxiety than your body needs adequate sleep and rest and is highly recommended that you get as much as 7-9 hours of sleep every night.

To be able to meet the required amount of sleep, follow these tips:

- Go to bed early and rise early. You can feel a more energized physical body when you get enough sleep at night and wake up for an early start.

- Turn off all lights and electronics before going to bed. It is known that electronic gadgets and devices released electromagnetic fields that have negative effects on our body. To release them, you need some grounding like taking a bath, walking barefoot on the ground and connecting with nature. It is also better if you can leave your electronic gadgets out of your room.

Visit your Physician

Generalized anxiety disorder or simple anxiety sometimes requires the intervention of medical practitioners through further treatment and evaluation outside of the shift in dietary lifestyle. See you doctor or those professional experts in mental health once the symptoms of anxiety become severe, cause you a lot of stress, and interfere with your daily life. Common anxiety symptoms include panic attacks, increased heart rate, nervousness, sweating, difficulty in concentration, and trembling. For a more severe type of anxiety that may require medical treatment, symptoms include suicidal attempts and constantly feeling that worries are interfering with your work and daily life.

Conclusion

Controlling your mind and unleashing its full power through rewiring your anxious thoughts and shifting to an effective dietary lifestyle will help you reduce panic attacks, fear, worries, and other anxiety-related symptoms if not prevent their occurrence.

It's not easy to control an anxious mind, and it needs long training of meditative exercises to shift its direction to a new one. For years, it had been used to habits that had somehow formed your behaviour and overall personality, and to be able to transform these habits, and you need to start with rewiring your thoughts and emotions, particularly the anxious ones.

Now that you are aware of how an anxious mind operates and that you can do something not only to control it but to unleash its full power to calm down unsettled thoughts and emotions, it's high time that you start acting on it.

Living with troublesome thinking and emotions can deprive you of a happy and successful life, and unless you take control of your anxious mind, it will continue to take full control of you.

Use you anxious mind's power to direct your anxiety and make it work to your advantage NOW!

Final Words

Thank you again for purchasing this book! I really hope this book is able to help you.

The next step is for you to **join our email newsletter** to receive updates on any upcoming new book releases or promotions. You can sign-up for free and as a bonus, you will also receive our "*7 Fitness Mistakes You Don't Know You're Making*" book! This bonus book breaks down many of the most common fitness mistakes and will demystify many of the complexities and science of getting into shape. Having all this fitness knowledge and science organized into an actionable step-by-step book will help you get started in the right direction in your fitness journey! To join our free email newsletter and grab your free book, please visit the link and signup: **www.hmwpublishing.com/gift**

Finally, if you enjoyed this book, then I would like to ask you for a favor, would you be kind enough to leave a review for this book? It would be greatly appreciated!

Thank you and good luck in your journey!

About the Co-Author

My name is George Kaplo; I'm a certified personal trainer from Montreal, Canada. I'll start off by saying I'm not the biggest guy you will ever meet and this has never really been my goal. In fact, I started working out to overcome my biggest insecurity when I was younger, which was my self-confidence. This was due to my height measuring only 5 foot 5 inches (168cm), it pushed me down to attempt anything I ever wanted to achieve in life. You may be going through some challenges right now, or you may simply want to get fit, and I can certainly relate.

For me personally, I was always kind of interested in the health & fitness world and wanted to gain some muscle due to the numerous bullying in my teenage years about my height and my overweight body. I figured I couldn't do anything about my height, but I sure can do something about how my body looked like. This was the beginning of my transformation journey. I had no idea where to start, but I just got started. I felt worried and afraid at times that other people would make fun of me for doing the exercises the wrong way. I always wished I had a friend that was next to me who was knowledgeable enough to help me get started and "show me the ropes."

After a lot of work, studying and countless trial and errors. Some people began to notice how I was getting more fit and how I was starting to form a keen interest in the topic. This led many friends and new faces to come to me and ask me for fitness advice. At first, it seemed odd when people asked me to help them get in shape. But what kept me going is when they started to see changes in their own body and told me it's the first time that they saw real results!

From there, more people kept coming to me, and it made me realize after so much reading and studying in this field that it did help me but it also allowed me to help others. I'm now a fully certified personal trainer and have trained numerous clients to date who have achieved amazing results.

Today, my brother Alex Kaplo (also a Certified Personal Trainer) and I own & operate this publishing venture, where we bring passionate and expert authors to write about health and fitness topics. We also run an online fitness website "HelpMeWorkout.com" and I would love to connect with by inviting you to visit the website on the following page and signing up to our e-mail newsletter (you will even get a free book).

Last but not least, if you are in the position I was once in and you want some guidance, don't hesitate and ask... I'll be there to help you out!

Your friend and coach,

George Kaplo
Certified Personal Trainer

Get another book for Free

I want to thank you for purchasing this book and offer you another book (just as long and valuable as this book), "Health & Fitness Mistakes You Don't Know You're Making", completely free.

Visit the link below to signup and receive it:

www.hmwpublishing.com/gift

In this book, I will break down the most common health & fitness mistakes, you are probably committing right now, and I will reveal how you can easily get in the best shape of your life!

In addition to this valuable gift, you will also have an opportunity to get our new books for free, enter giveaways, and receive other valuable emails from me. Again, visit the link to sign up:

www.hmwpublishing.com/gift

Copyright 2017 by HMW Publishing - All Rights Reserved.

This document by HMW Publishing owned by the A&G Direct Inc company, is geared towards providing exact and reliable information in regards to the topic and issue covered. The publication is sold with the idea that the publisher is not required to render accounting, officially permitted, or otherwise, qualified services. If advice is necessary, legal or professional, a practiced individual in the profession should be ordered.

From a Declaration of Principles which was accepted and approved equally by a Committee of the American Bar Association and a Committee of Publishers and Associations.

In no way is it legal to reproduce, duplicate, or transmit any part of this document in either electronic means or in printed format. Recording of this publication is strictly prohibited, and any storage of this document is not allowed unless with written permission from the publisher. All rights reserved.

The information provided herein is stated to be truthful and consistent, in that any liability, in terms of inattention or otherwise, by any usage or abuse of any policies, processes, or directions contained within is the solitary and utter responsibility of the recipient reader. Under no circumstances will any legal responsibility or blame be held against the publisher for any reparation, damages, or monetary loss due to the information herein, either directly or indirectly.

The information herein is offered for informational purposes solely, and is universal as so. The presentation of the information is without contract or any type of guarantee assurance.

The trademarks that are used are without any consent, and the publication of the trademark is without permission or backing by the trademark owner. All trademarks and brands within this book are for clarifying purposes only and are the owned by the owners themselves, not affiliated with this document.

For more great books visit:

HMWPublishing.com

www.ingramcontent.com/pod-product-compliance
Lightning Source LLC
Chambersburg PA
CBHW071912070526
44583CB00016B/1957